THE INTERNAL OBJECTS

THE INTERNAL OBJECTS

SZU-HAN HO

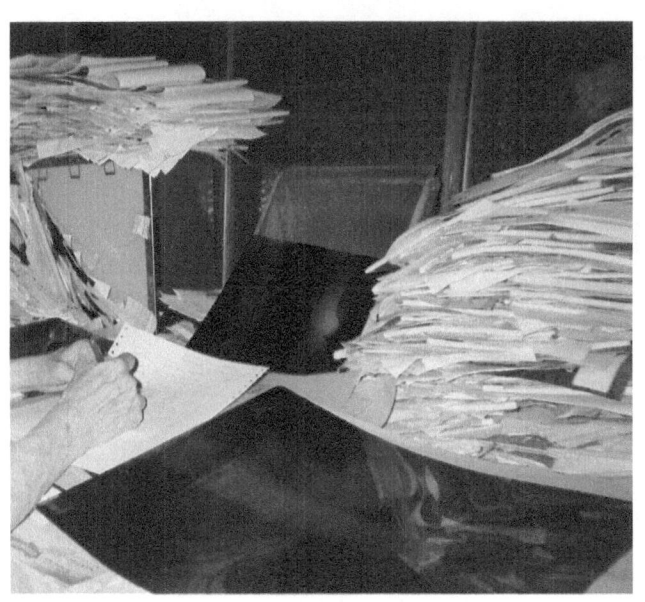

. . . .

RADIOLOGY JOURNAL, SEPTEMBER 176 (3); reporting on the successful practice of remembered classmate, who started a clinic in Honduras. The classmate had always been sloppy, thought K. It was no wonder he was practicing in the Third World. Semi-gloss cover art of hospital building and pale jonquils. *Remember to fact-check citations in paper "Breast MRI Technology... The Coming Wave?"; contact the editors about typo on page 56,* "patella" *misspelled as* "paletta." New, thinner paper stock. This issue addressed to retired director; inside of back cover—a satisfactory place to write down the number of days since last delivery of PET radioisotope. Must remember where it is written. The young physicist needs regular reminding. Side-effects of contrast chemistry discovered to have no harmful impact in five-year study. *Tingling, warming, and the sensation of needing to urinate.*

UMBRELLA; gray handle, white aster flowers on baby blue; one broken stretcher rib (not the double-jointed collapsible type that would fit in a handbag). A metal rod from an unwound artificial flower stem, last seen on top of newspaper stack, could be used to make this repair. Scattered Showers in the forecast for tomorrow, A Few Clouds today, Hi 71 Lo 46, 42% humidity, barometric pressure 1031.0 mb. K imagined this one belonging to a woman like the housewife in her 50s who had been haggling for monkfish.

CONCISE RUSSIAN-ENGLISH DICTIONARY, REVISED EDITION; published by Oxford University Press. Dog-eared on EVO-FAL. Tattered corner back cover. Back jacket: *"This dictionary provides coverage of 120,000 words and phrases, and over 190,000 translations. It includes completely up-to-date treatment of contemporary Russian and English, including* amniocentesis, global warming, information superhighway, multimedia, streetwise, and time-share."

NEWSPAPER CLIPPING; story of a man with six fingers on both right and left hand, showing off his medical anomaly for reporters on B2. *A ring on each ring finger.* Photocopying images from the dailies were a part of K's routine in the hospital mailroom, where the newspaper rods hung on racks like laundry. No specific criteria for the images he chose. Certain pictures were like a punch line. Some he put in an envelope to mail to one of his sons, others joined the tower of loose clippings on the desk. *Be sure to mail this to B, who as a ten-year-old, had written a story about a six-fingered protagonist.* K still kept a copy of this story and accompanying illustrations in his files.

....

NYLON STRING; bright pink, twisted mason's line. The right length for a plumb bob. Taken from package addressed to a Mr. W, sent from an overseas address in Southeast Asia. Full of blankets and clothing, probably not unlike the dresses K used to send to his granddaughter. Smiling, foundation-covered saleswomen at the department store would help him to pick out clothing to suit a 15-month-old baby girl with almond eyes and tiny mouth.

WHITE HANDKERCHIEF; now yellowing, un-embroidered, most likely owned by a sweaty, middle-management-type. K thanked his lucky genome for the fact that he was not a heavy perspirer. A nightly wipe with a damp cloth sufficed to feel refreshed. During the peak of summer in the urban heat island, he saw sweat soaking through suits before the workday had begun. Few people carried handkerchiefs anymore. Even fewer wore suits to work. His own suit jacket had been custom tailored in 1958; it seemed to be growing larger, so that he felt like a kid playing dress-up. In the winter, he wore thicker wool sweater vests to fill out the jacket, but in the summer there was little to be done. The white coat could be worn over the jacket. More than one nurse was known to notice how it flattered his tall, lean frame.

BROWN PAPER LUNCH SACK; came with an egg salad sandwich, chips, and apple. Day-old sandwiches were half-off, the chips satisfyingly salty. Small oval stains on two bottom edges of the sack, probably from the egg salad. The Red Delicious should not be called an apple. The cultivar was the definition of mealy, K thought, and could be traced back to Iowa around 1880. A century later, three out of every four apples coming out of Washington was RD. From Johnny Appleseed to government bailout of the apple growers in the nineties. This particular sack was an object that could be flattened, stacked, and tied in bulging bundles of 100, perhaps with the newly acquired NYLON STRING.

POP Aluminum Rivets; pack of 100, 3.2mm head diameter, 8mm length, 3.4mm fixing hole diameter. The choice for a finished look to both sides of any project.

Men's Lightweight jacket; Big and Tall size, eggshell with navy blue piping. 100 percent polyester shell. Made in El Salvador.

....

Oscillating Fan; K knew instantly and from afar that this one was a real find. Walking in the late afternoon, after the yard sale rejects were left out on the sidewalk, he couldn't believe his luck. A small tabletop model with bright blue translucent fins inside a stainless radial shell. The buttons were rectangular, opaque blue blocks with thumb-sized concavities that caught with a confident click. The kind of high-quality goods they'd made when the country still excelled in light industrial products. K was sure he could get this one going again. He especially enjoyed the way that no two buttons stayed down at once, no matter how fast a consecutive push. A simple logic structure and a credit to the engineer. Some blender settings gave a

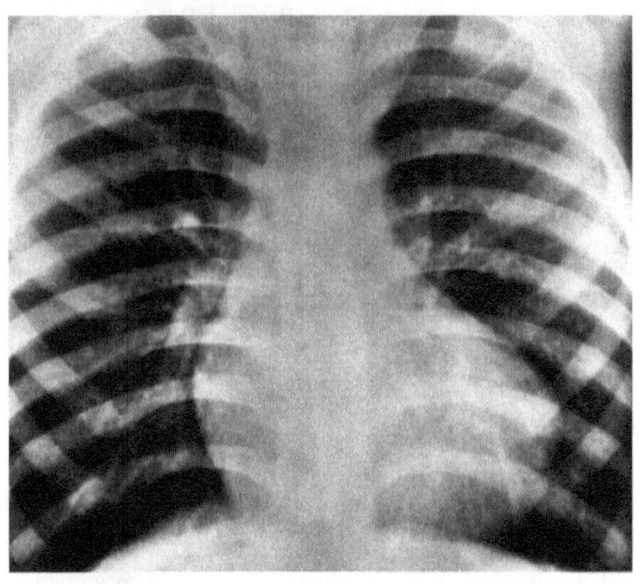

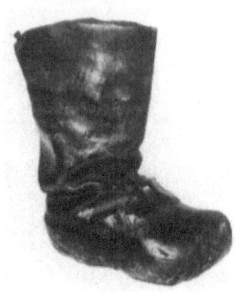

Fig. 1. 'Boot-shaped Heart Sign (Coeur En Sabot).' Boot-shaped heart showing 'Pulmonary Stenosis: p, apex of the left heart; p'. apex of the right heart.'

similar satisfaction. He lamented the new designs that deprived one of real button-pushing; shallow clicks and digital beeps were a paltry substitute and a regression for the sensory experience of the masses. Oscillating fans of the last five years—monopod skyscrapers rotating on a palsied footing—looked ill-adapted with such high centers of gravity. One was lucky if they lasted past two consecutive summers. Still, K saved the broken ones for the parts.

WOODEN FOLDING CHAIR; thin dimension lumber and crisscrossed backing, a thin metal plate with an embossed number. This had belonged to the girls' high school on the next block. After he'd brought it home he realized that it reminded him of something unpleasant, but what. A replacement could be found for the missing bolt and wing nut at the bottom hinge (surely something suitable in the DRAWER OF HARDWARE, BATTERIES & RECEIPTS). A length of wood, electrical cord, and duct tape would make a clever splint to hold the broken leg together. His growing family of surgically-restored furniture gave immeasurable gratification. Creativity found full expression: a leg from one chair grafted onto another, the broken leaf of a table replaced with the sawed lid of a rubber bin. Each piece was its own exercise in triage and surgical reconstruction. If he managed to salvage a damaged arm or lower leg from the orthopedists, he could use actual human prosthetics. K dreamt that the rescued sofas, folding chairs, stools, and baby cribs were walking around the house, convalescing up and down stairs, and that he was a resident in charge of this Post-Op Recovery Unit.

CARDBOARD CAKE BOX; from a recent birthday or retirement. His own retirement party had been full of unrecognized faces, smiling and cheering something or someone but not him. Where had they managed to find this many people who were glad to see him go? They had no clue what it would mean, that there would be no one to see to it that mistakes made by residents and first-years were caught before a catastrophe. The world had stopped paying proper attention: faulty engineering on large infrastructure projects caused bridges to collapse, chemicals meant for plastics in baby formula and dog food, mutant amphibians created by agricultural run-off. K vowed never to let up on attention. No aberration in the medium of x-ray film escaped his razor sharp eyesight and intuition, cultivated from years of staring at the black-and-gray celluloid apparitions. His dull wax pencil prefigured the surgeon's knife. Here was the department head saying something to the crowd and holding up a glass. *Roomful of faces now turning to him, smiling and waiting.*

....

GLASS TABLETOP; ⅜ in. x 5 ft. x 3 ft. Beveled edges. Very thick, very heavy (was it coffee tabletop, coffee/table/top?). To be moved into place as carefully as he could manage alone (he'd dropped and shattered more than one of these unwieldy plates). Maneuvering it through the narrow doorway and over multiple thresholds into the back room was not an easy task. For a moment, K thought that he might be forced to ask the neighbors' teenage son for help. The kid was always glad to oblige in exchange for a few explicit magazines from the pile of NEW ARRIVALS. For now, the large sheet would come in handy for leaning against the wall to contain a growing stack of bulk mailings.

SEW-ON SNAPS; (12) ¼ in. diameter, 100 percent nylon. Use to hold overlapping edges together.

OIL PAINTING, WITH FRAME; an amateur painting in oil of a familiar cartoon bear. He recognized the character because his grandchildren had insisted on watching the adventures of the credulous bear for whole afternoons during their visits when they were young. He found the world of these forest friends fascinating. He was sympathetic to the philosophical musing of the slow, fat pooh. The neurotic pig and rabbit he identified with as well, but the energetic lisping tiger who threw everything into chaos he found disagreeable. Such persons he observed in life had a similar cluelessness to their actions and were pathologically ecstatic. He felt hapless around these people. The artist had painted the bear walleyed with an elongated snout, but still, there was a recognizable intent and an appropriate naiveté.

. . . .

BLACK PLASTIC COMB; couple of tines missing here and there at the higher octaves. *Always did like the sound of the plink-plinky glissando.* When he tried to give this one a

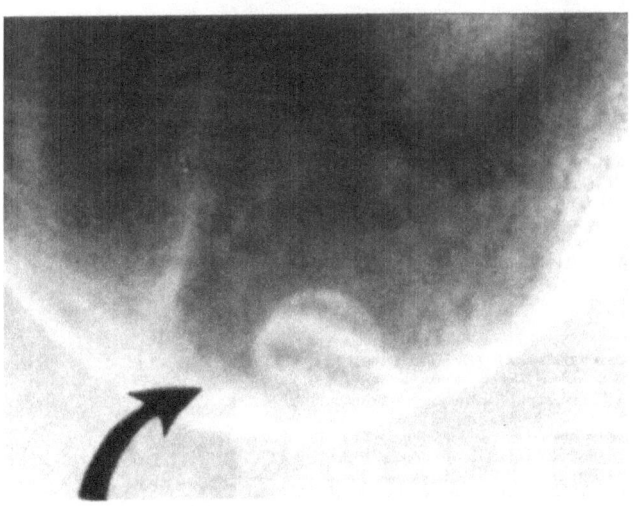

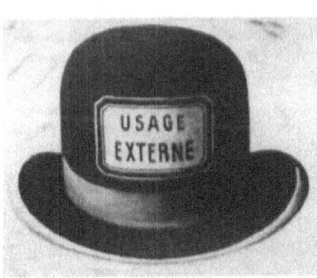

Fig. 2. 'Bowler Hat Sign.' Intermediate type of polyp with 'hat sign.' Differentiation of true polypoid tumors of the colon from extraneous material.

run, a few more broke in a brittle shower, but the missing tines made for even more interesting harmonies, a pentatonic arpeggio. K had very little use for a comb these days, but it was one of those mundane necessities he assumed would always be in ubiquitous production. The handle of Mother's wooden comb carried oil stains from frequent use on the three tangled heads of her children. Combing was a time of brief bliss. Standing before the mirror in the mornings before being sent to school, he had her undivided attention. She was determined to send out into the world little ambassadors with impeccable scores, well-pressed uniforms, and above all, neatly parted hair. He carried his own comb for fixing the part again before heading home. His older brother was even more bookish and quiet than he, but defended himself better in sticky situations with schoolmates. At some point in middle school, around the time that his academic performance floated him to the top of the class, K started to inch above his brother. Collective groaning when he was saddled to a kickball team meant little since K knew he was useless on the playing field and might even be left alone. The teams switched sides while he waited in outfield through entire games, oblivious of the rules and content to calculate in his head probabilities of the ball's trajectory at various angles. This particular plastic comb was from the Bureau of Weights and Measures, embossed with a seal and painted in a misregistered white.

1-GALLON HUMIDIFIER; chalky white plastic base. Top-heavy translucent blue cover. Whisper-quiet operation and a removable filter.

BOOK OF CARBON PAPER; 100 sheets. A life without carbon paper was a cruel and unfathomable idea to K. What other medium could claim to sacrifice itself for the sake of reproduction? The notes he made for each patient file all needed to be copied for the clinic and the referring doctor. His own copy stayed securely in booklet form while the originals he sent back with the film. Each delicate black leaf was precious and to be used as many times as possible. A booklet of 100 carbon sheets had the limp weight of a very thick head of hair. Two Russian physicists recently won the Nobel for creating a single-carbon-atom-thick sheet that was both the thinnest material in the world and one of the strongest. K savored the way that the blackness of his paper gave way to pressure in becoming a medium of transfer. If he wrote over previously used sections, the ghosted writing appeared in the new copy. This material was definitely becoming scarcer, *was even on its way out,* which made harvesting whatever he could all the more urgent. On one occasion he had lucked upon a closing office supply store and bought out the entire stock. An expenditure that would more than cover itself in coming years.

STANDARD PREMIUM STAPLES; box of 5000. ¼ in. finely honed chisel points for maximum penetration.

....

LOBSTER CRACKER; 6 ¼ in., soft red grip handle. Useful for breaking open shellfish without destroying the edible insides. Ridged interior holds crab or lobster while cracking. Ideal for nuts too.

ROAD MAP OF CITY OF SAN DIEGO; published by the American Automobile Association. K did not know anyone who lived on the West Coast. His youngest son M had lived in a suburb of another Sun Belt city. K himself had never lived anywhere other than the place of his birth. Didn't like to travel. There was the occasional overnight train ride for a conference, but otherwise, he stuck to his route from the hospital to the neighborhood and back.

His last time on an airplane had been decades ago, in the days when air travel was still a luxury. The medical school

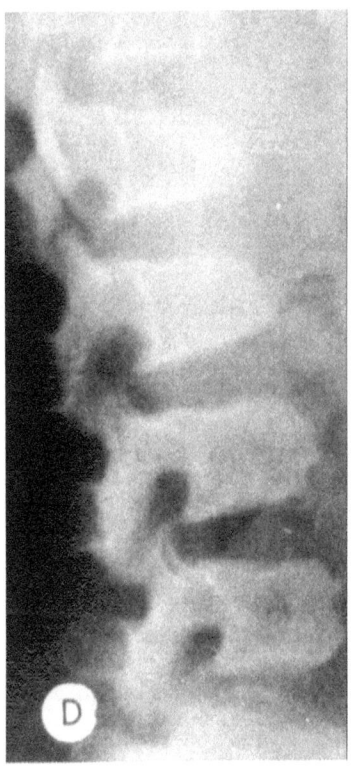

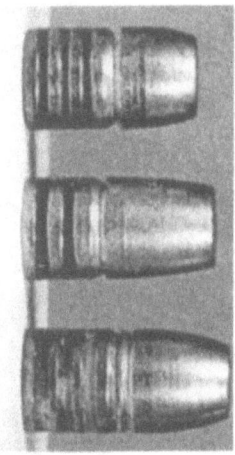

Fig. 3. 'Bullet-shaped Vertebrae.' Smallness and pinching of the ventral ends of the first and second lumbar bodies into rounded bullen-nosed deformities. Achondroplasia of pelvis and lumbosacral spine.

had flown him out for training on stereoscopic technique. He'd been enthralled in the airport, imagining himself to be a singular atom bouncing along this network of speed and privilege. Strapped in for takeoff, he was transfixed looking out the window and thinking of Bernoulli's equation. The plane began to lift itself smoothly off of the tarmac. It sped along with one toe still on the ground, until it had fully defied its own weight and was airborne. He sighed and sat back to feel his stomach drop and head swoon. The plane gave a jolt. He felt the fuselage flex in different directions and heard the seams creak. The stewardess quickly turned around and scuttled away. In an instant, he felt his throat constricting and his lungs tightening, gasping for oxygen from the abruptly thin air. He heard a high-pitched yelp lost in the muffled roar and realized it had come from him. He grabbed and tried to hold onto the armrest to steady himself, but the seats were in league with the rest of the plane and jostled back and forth despite his best effort. He felt the urgent need to vomit and started to fumble with the seat belt. The colleague sitting next to him extended an arm across his chest, saying *Whoa, stay put. Just a bit of turbulence. It'll be over just like that.* A tunnel formed and began rapidly closing in. BLACK.

He bought a lone train ticket on the return trip home, though it came out of his own pocket and required an extra overnight stay. it was a small price to pay for maintaining firm contact with the Earth. He'd been given a heavy tranquilizer after he awoke from passing out, realized he was still in the air, and started flailing his arms while screaming. His colleagues held him down until he passed out for the second time, and when they finally landed, he had to be carried off of the plane barely conscious by two radiologists from the host institution. He swore he would never get on another, and he stuck to that promise.

Maps, K found, were a far better way to explore the world. Ideal, really. Without the low-pressure cabins or flexing fuselages or radiation exposure, he could move through the streets in detailed maps with abandon, from the zoos to shopping malls, to the boardwalk performers. He knew where to buy local crafts, what time of year was best for whale watching, and which museums had free days. Cartoonish tourist maps, aerial photos, travel guides, encyclopedias, and television shows all informed his imagined adventures. His knowledge was so extensive that he could make recommendations to colleagues and family members for all major cities, and if they traveled to places he'd never heard of, he would promptly dive into research.

He never did visit that suburb of the Sun Belt city.

PICTURE FRAME; 13 in. x 19 in. brushed metal picture frame. Could house a diploma nicely.

STETHOSCOPE; a missing earplug on the left side made it painful to actually use, but the diaphragm and chest piece were still good. The color of the bakelite, a faded green, brought to mind the memory of all of the hospital fixtures forty years ago, before the old building had been gutted and remodeled with mottled surfaces of unidentifiable material.

WAX PENCIL; white, with about 5 in. or so left. To pull the white thread that unwound the paper exposing the waxy core was a special thrill. Found behind the chair in a waiting room. Wax on celluloid reminded him of greasing a baking pan with a stick of butter, always his task when Mother was baking her breads. The goal was to coat every single part of the edges and corners of the rectangular baking dish with a geometrically-similar, blunt instrument. He abused the stick of butter in the attempt to be thorough, whittling it down until there was nothing but a palm-shaped smudge. Still, she praised his work. *All-the-better with that much butter!* She would let him take the rest of the wax paper to lick and to draw on. He slid his pointer finger around to form oily stick men and figure eights.

STACK OF MAGAZINES; including Time (December 30, 1961), Field and Stream (Apr 1988, Jan 1972, Mar 1987), Reader's Digest (Jan-Dec 1970), Farmer's Almanac (1985), Cosmopolitan (July-Dec 1989), Gentleman's Quarterly (Nov 1988-July 1989), Vogue (Mar 1972-Feb 1974, Sep 1976). Quality of paper stock and finish quite varied. K was months into an analysis of facial expressions (What degree of happiness is being expressed by the subject? 0 Neutral/Pensive—10 Extreme/Ecstatic). The last time S had visited, however, the entire data set had secretly been thrown out, to K's extreme dismay.

. . . .

PACK OF PAPERCLIPS; 200-pack of gold, #1-size clips. Never-before-seen gold paper clips! Staring at a handful, K thought of the one and only time that his father had taken him to the office. Two bony hands holding on tightly, they walked through a noisy factory to a long, narrow, carpeted room against the far wall of

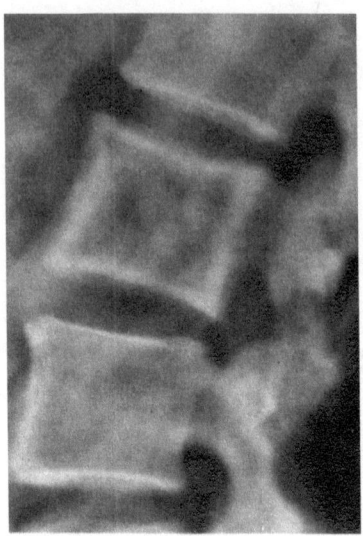

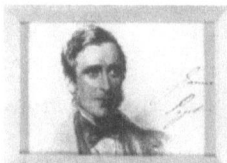

Fig. 4. 'Picture Frame Sign.' Lateral spine radiograph with typical picture-frame appearance due to Paget's disease.

the cavernous building. K was to sit down at the edge of the desk, which was in a row of other desks along a line facing the same direction. Ladies who walked by leaving a sickly sweet smell in their wake smiled at him. He was given a stack of paper clips, a mechanical pencil, eraser, and papers to do multiplication tables. He was up to the 14s, and Mother was fond of bragging to other family members. His father, who he remembered as always walking with his head bent slightly forward of his body, looked even more terrapin here. The office ladies kept bringing stacks of paper and leaving them on the desk. He showed K how to make the paper clips into little "frogs" that jumped high into the air when dropped. *Two hundred gold frogs leaping at split-second intervals.*

MECHANICAL PENCIL; black, faceted body with chrome clip. 0.7 mm lead. Rubber eraser completely worn or missing. One piece of lead rattled inside.

PLASTIC DRINKING STRAWS; (6) still in paper. K had observed a little girl playing solitary games with straws at a restaurant table full of adults, chattering away. The girl was making "worms" out of the scrunched-up paper. She dipped her plastic straw into a glass of water and held it in a vacuum with her thumb until she carefully and deliberately placed a single drop of water on the paper, making it expand and squirm. K grinned, thinking it was an ingenious material exploration. He grabbed extra straws to try it for himself later.

COFFEE GRINDER; small, cylindrical black body. Lid-activated, but motor no longer working. Smell of coffee beans, clove, and peppercorns.

PAPER MILK CARTON; used, flattened, stacked. The 4 in. x 4 in. square footprint of these pint boxes made for very good collapse. They were a ledger of his daily breakfast ritual in the hospital cafeteria. Even though lactose wreaked havoc on his intestinal tract, K took his place in line behind the tired family members and OR nurses in faded scrubs to buy his daily milk carton and serving of balled melons. The paper boxes sat askance in a tub of disc-shaped ice. Beads of condensation mingled with dried drops of glue that held the paperboard together. K loved the complex geometries of the folded volume: a pyramid atop a cube opened into a parallelogram that could be flattened into a neatly proportioned rectangle. Other MDs rarely frequented the cafeteria. They preferred the designated doctors' lounge where the fruit was inevitably fresher, the entrées hotter, and the conversations muffled by the thick carpeting. But in the lounge the milk came in thick pint glasses rather than cartons. Why pass up an opportunity to mark the day with the wonders of automated paperboard assembly? Waiting to pay, he fantasized about relentless precision of the machine that stamped, cut, folded, and glued the little volume together. And then there was the act of opening. How did they manage to apply just the right mix of adhesive to allow for his perfect tearing into a rhomboidal spout? K might have been very happy as a materials engineer for a company such as this one, LIQUID SOLUTIONS, INC., but pondering engineering problems of disposable life would have to remain reserved for pastime pleasure.

2-GALLON PLASTIC BUCKET; cerulean with geologic white rings of calcified deposit that ran up the insides in varying time scales. A white plastic cylinder for a handle, wrapped around the rigid, light-gauge steel wire. A subtle spout. There was a shiny potato chip bag corner stuck to the bottom and a dead roach. The bucket was collected near a dumpster, although he later admitted to himself that someone could conceivably have been cleaning and left it there temporarily. He did, however, have an arguable need. The roof in the back room leaked during heavy rains, and he used every available volume to contain the flow. The ten or so pots and buckets he had set out during the last rain were full to the brim. Since the water next to the storage room had been shut off years ago, the stored rainwater happened to provide a convenient supply for washing. Mosquitoes bred in the summer months, so he topped each one with a plastic bag, held in place with string around the mouth of the container.

. . . .

DELUXE 2-HOLE PUNCH WITH CHIP DRAWER; able to punch up to 50 sheets of 20 lb. paper. Jam resistant.

20-INCH BOX FAN; light gray housing, white plastic grid and blades. The dust had collected in a predictable gradient on each cell of the grid and along the fan blades in a curve that traced the movement of air across. It was surprisingly heavy for plastic. Old enough to be brittle. The electric plug was hanging tenuously from its cord, with the wiring exposed and on the verge of decapitation. He plugged it in anyway. It hummed to life slowly, and he remembered sitting in front of one just like this for hours, singing into it. *The fan duetted with him in the overwhelming air,*

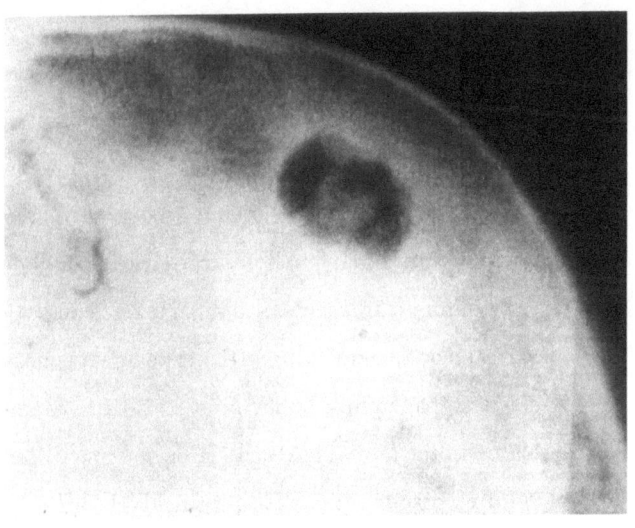

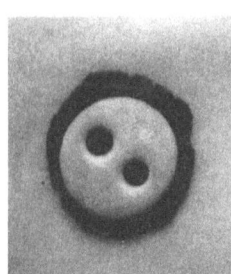

Fig. 5. 'Button sequestrum.' The osteolytic lesion in the right parietal bone involves both tables of the calvarium and contains a 'button' of bone.

chopping his OOOOO–oooooEEEEEE–eeeeeeAAAAAs into digital units. Long vowels shifted into harmonic overtones. Sweltering summer days in which he sat alone, while his brother and sister were at the uncle's house that he refused to go to. Mother let him stay in if he locked himself inside and promised not to leave for the six hours she was away cleaning other people's homes. K found company in collaborations with household appliances: singing his fan duet, slicing newsprint with a blender, testing static on the television with tissues and nylon hose. The refrigerator door became the site for an archaeological dig. He once built an entire landscape of ancient ruins with his personal collection of magnets, paperclips, bobby pins, and nails. When Mother came home and saw his creation, she marvelled at his empire, discovering castle ruins and dinosaur skulls peeping from the various corners. She opened the door gingerly for weeks to avoid disturbing the site.

BLENDER; black plastic base, plastic cord, plastic buttons, scratched plastic jar, plastic lid, Model # 51101B. Broken metal blades.

UMBRELLA; compact, travel-size. Canopy open to 39 in. arc. Red lines in geometric pattern on black. Stretcher ribs all intact.

Samsonite Suitcase; maroon cloth, threadbare at three out of four of the front corners. Broken zipper. Handle stuck midway in the out position. Suitcases took up a lot of space but could be used to store things, like stacks of paper. He would try to fix the zipper. Zippers held the world together (until they inevitably broke). K had heard that the YKK headquarters in Tokyo was in the shape of a zipper. The largest zipper manufacturer in the world also makes fenestration systems. *An onomatopoeic name was key to commercial success.* This universal fastener. How many thousands of miles of zipping occurred each day? You could almost tell by the feel of each one how much longer it had until its teeth jammed. He felt a sudden painful pinch in his pointer finger while trying to make the suitcase close. The skin broke easily and he bled, leaving a darker spot on the already-maroon weave.

Engine Gaskets; rubber or plastic polymer, compelling variation in positive and negative shapes.

Bicycle Helmet: electric blue streaks on black. Inside foam torn. Dial-fit retention system allowing for easy, on-the-fly adjustment. During his first year in college, his son M had come home on a gas scooter. It became the chosen mode of transport everywhere M went, running errands for his mother, meeting up with friends to study and later to go for a drink. There was a small compartment in the seat where he could carry things, sometimes gracing the family dog with a ride. M's helmet was a glittery reflective black. Not scuffed like this one, which had clearly seen a few collisions. As a father, it struck K as a rather resourceful and convenient way for a young modern man to get around the congested city, even if the young modern man was seen driving a bit too fast. Still, K admired his son for being self-sufficient in such an untroubled way. K would sit in the back of cabs during rush hour, experiencing eyelid spasms with every flip of the meter and watching cyclists and scooterists zipping by. M was often tinkering with the bike when his father came home from work.

. . . .

TABLE LAMP; a shade of orange rarely duplicated in newer appliances, except in the intentionally retro. Corded wire. A single large knob that switched on and off with an easy 30-degree clockwise turn and click. Low wattage incandescent bulb, smaller than the standard. Sticky film and dust buildup around entire shade and base. Still working, although he probably wouldn't use it anyway. More lighting was not needed, since K would not allow his power usage to exceed the fixed amount that he had maintained for at least fifteen years (since S had left). They were mostly fluorescents in the house; they seemed to attract fewer bugs anyway. The single tube swung solitary over his armchair where he did all of his reading, television watching, and napping. The rest of the house was dark.

Wite-Out Brand Correction Tape; contoured design for ultimate comfort. No shadow produced on copies or faxes.

General Purpose Tarp; 12 ft. x 16 ft., water and tear resistant plastic polyethylene material. Blue color. Great for camping, construction, agriculture, boating, landscaping and roof covering.

Mason Jar; 8-oz., ideal size for canning in small quantities. There had been a constant assortment in the kitchen when he was a child. The ones in the fridge could persist there for years: crab apple jellies, caramels, pickled vegetables. These sometimes became fascinating cultures, experiments for watching spore growth. Delicate bluish-

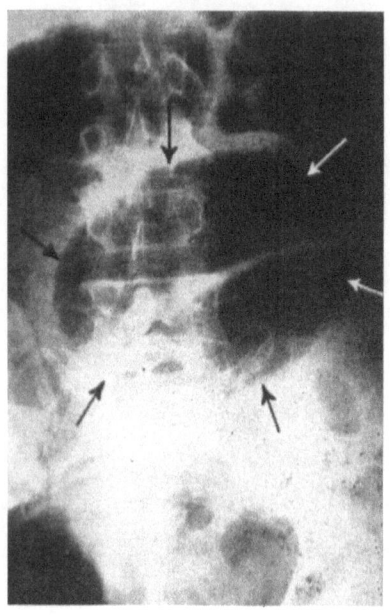

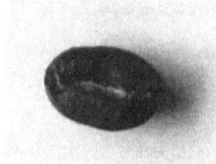

Fig. 6. 'Coffee Bean Sign.' Operation revealed a gas-distended, incarcerated loop, obstructed at two points by postoperative adhesions. The roentgen findings in strangulating obstructions of the small bowel.

whitish dandelions grew into anemones.

LEGAL PERFORATED WRITING PAD; 15 lb. paper, 8½ in. x 14 in.
50 sheets per pad. Smooth writing surface providing
skip-free writing.

....

ARTIFICIAL FLOWERS; assortment of once-white silk
daisies. An ancient feeling flashed. The dust on those fake
petals. Mother had been gone for three days, though this
was not unusual. The three children were left alone. They
kept up with their homework, and K was to make sure his
sister got to and from school safely. Late on the fourth day,
he was playing a paper cut-out game with some Jehovah's
Witness tracts. Their older brother was locked in his room
with an insect collection. Beetles were the latest
fascination. The field behind their house was a breeding
ground and battlefield for at least ten different species,
iridescently equipped with front-end loaders, rollers, and
jackhammers. Dung beetles feed solely on the feces of
other animals. One particular dung beetle makes its found

feces into a spherical ball at least fifty times its own weight and rolls it away to keep it safely from other beetles. K made a snowflake out of beetle-shaped cutouts.

They heard footsteps down the hallway, muffled voices, and a key in the lock. When Mother came in, she was with an uncle and two men K had never seen before. They brought the cold in with them on their breaths. The sudden crowding in the house masked the silence that the adults were doing their best to keep at bay.

K concentrated on the vivid purple of Mother's scarf while she spoke.

It was something that happened at work, he heard. His father had been moved to another part of the company. A man at the office who had been laid off a week before came to the floor where his father worked and attacked him. A large knife. K pictured the long, gleaming one that the fishmonger at the market used to gut and filet the snapper that Mother bought on Tuesdays. The attacker and the fishmonger came together in K's mind: a choleric man in his 50s with a unusual facial hair wearing a long coat stained with browns and reds that flew up as he lunged toward his father, diminutive. Something about the word "redundant." They said that the man directed all of his rage against the company at an innocent, aging accountant. For a long time, K thought that the word "redundant" implied vengeance. The man had screamed unrepeatable names as he ran out into the street and was subsequently hit by oncoming traffic.

Ever since the funeral, the house was always full of flowers (and dust) and people and the dishes they brought over. People K had never seen before gave him a look and talked in a way that seemed to K to refer generically to someone else's "loved one." Mother welcomed and thanked every guest for the sympathies. As far as he could tell, she always remained dry-eyed. Over the following year, K's paper snowflakes contained increasingly complex tessalations of beetles and fish. The beetles would wrestled each other, or engulf the fish with their pincers, or the two species would play king-of-the-mountain for the snowflake corners.

To Go Plastic Containers; (4) 6 in. x 8½ in. x 2 in. Injection-molded polypropylene engineered for heat and cold resistance. Clear top, black bottom. Thick-walled, able to withstand temperatures between 0 degrees and 250 degrees Fahrenheit.

. . . .

As Yet Unresolved, Questions:

Q: Why can't you have a phone line on the moon?

Q: Why, really, do humans stand on two legs instead of four?

Q: Does a snail have consciousness?

Q: Why are there 24 hours in a day?

Q: Why are legal pads yellow?

Q: Why are there no "B" batteries?

Q: What happens to an astronaut's blood when he cuts himself in space?

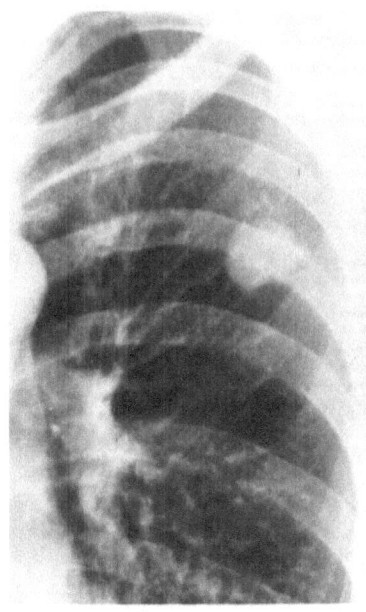

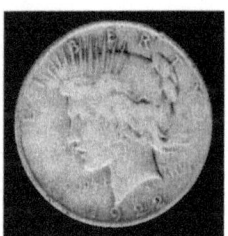

Fig. 7. 'Coin Lesion.' Chest radiograph showing solitary pulmonary nodule.

....

OVERSIZED RUBBER BANDS; (20) thick, short bands with very high resistance. Assorted colors.

RUBBER STAMP PADS; one side with red ink, the other with black. Both nearly dried but with some hope of resurrection in this humidity. *Now where were those stamps made from little B's drawings?* There was one of a small cat, very cleverly drawn with the head and body tapering to a thin point at the neck, no collar. A pastry-tube creature of smooth curves and jagged ends for a tail, ears, and paws. His six year-old son was delighted with the custom stamp that K had ordered from these drawings, an endlessly repeatable facsimile that he then used to populate surfaces with entire cat colonies and then, for years, as his signature on all drawings and homework. In the evening when K was reading film, B sat next to him creating hybrid creatures made of more pastry-tube forms: a pigeon's head and wings on a tiger's body, a chimpanzee with armadillo shell and claws. A rodent-goat munching on a boy's head of hair.

They made K chuckle out loud.

Spiral Pads; curled at the bottom edges. With writing on the first five pages, notes written in gratuitously sloppy scribbles from a lecture on *Ethnic Variance in the Epidemiology of Scoliosis.* Someone's forgotten notepad at the talk, where K had relished asking questions and challenging the speaker on the link between race and idiopathic scoliosis.

Box of T-pins; 1½ in. long, some quite rusted but most intact. He practiced draftsmanship secretly for years when he had imagined becoming an inventor/engineer. He stole the T-pins that Mother used in her knitting and macramé to pin-up axonometric drawings of robotic assembly arm prototypes. The T-pins showed up later in high school biology classes for dissection. They held the skin and organs of the fetal pig in a delicate exploded order, there to be deciphered and understood as diagrams.

Pin-Cushion; a red and segmented stuffed citrus, encircled by a ring of twelve round-bodied, pig-tailed little Orientalist children. Each one had a brightly-colored satin body that straddled the giant cushion with arms and legs that came to a point. Much like the pastry-

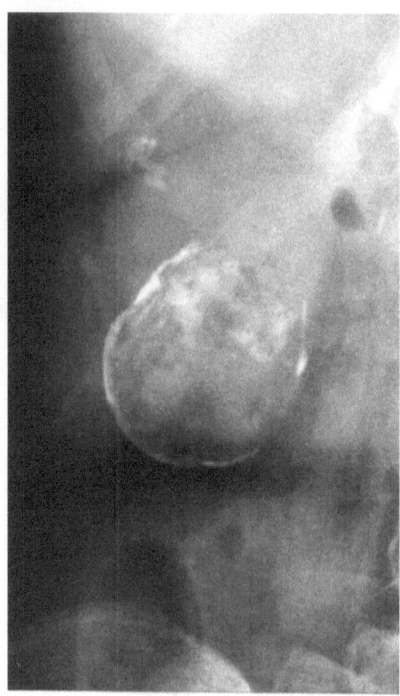

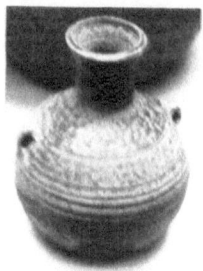

Fig. 8. 'Porcelain Gall-bladder.' Abdominal radiograph showing calcified gallbladder.

tube characters. It was identical to one that S had used when hemming K's pants.

....

CALLIGRAPHER'S PEN NIB; he could no longer picture the old man. There were no photographs around the house; there never had been. The large portrait that had been part of the service was wrapped in newsprint and stored deeply away along with the few boxes of his personal effects. He remained only a vague outline to K, who tried to remember facial features in more detail as he stared at the fountain pen that had been given to him on his fifth birthday (a lavish gift, but for a precocious child). The pen had a weight and girth that he had liked to feel in his small hands. K started to collect other pens, assaying and classifying all of the different variables that went into their construction. The hollow lightweight plastic of a cheap BIC, the spring resistance of a bright yellow clicking pen given away by the local bank, a solid stainless steel ballpoint with a rotating click action. The precise fluidity of a

Japanese-made 0.5 mm microball.

PHOTO FRAMES; (2) 6 in. x 9 in. empty, thin, and wooden. K inserted the photograph of himself posing with two spandex-clad Russian female acrobatic performers, taken five years ago at a fund-raising dinner. He would put it on the shelf next to his only other photographs, one of his grandson L as an 18-month-old holding a blue terry cloth stuffed bear. Another one taken in the front room with the two older boys standing and facing the camera without smiling as S sat with their youngest on her lap. The last time he had spoken to his grandson was a brief phone call over six months ago. (He did not like to stay on the phone for more than three minutes at a time. As with the electric bill, he imposed a strict monthly maximum usage). *L, sounding as though he was calling from the street, was in town for a conference and did he have time to meet for dinner?* But dinner for K had already been planned out: leftover casserole from the hospital cafeteria and a piece of fruit. The food would spoil if it sat uneaten for one more night, *So no, he was very sorry he could not meet for dinner tonight.* Perhaps next time. *How is your health? Are you satisfied with work? Very good. Goodbye.* Click. Two minutes and sixteen seconds, according to the clock hanging above the telephone.

K rather enjoyed seeing his grandson, actually. Their visits were, in fact, usually very pleasant. The last time they had met, K spent three hours with him discussing the difference between Newtonian and Leibnizian calculus. He simply had his plans. Last minute surprises were extremely unwelcome intrusions, would change the entire rhythm with repercussions lasting for days. Everyone knew this; thus, family members were accustomed to giving fair warning before visits. It did not help things that for many years after she had left, S continued to drop in purposefully unannounced to do her "organizing:" wholesale, indiscriminate, destructive, devastating events in which roomfuls of things were carted out and discarded to unknown yards and recycling centers. K was dejected after these episodes but refused to give her the satisfaction of a response. And, in fact, it drove her mad that he did not seem to care but continued to bring his objects home. S left before she felt the collapse of a distinction between the inner world and the outer.

BOX OF 1-GALLON ZIPLOC BAGS; (40) clear, 1.75 ml storage bags. Double zipper seal.

18-IN. ROLL OF BROWN PAPER; a sour, wet smell. K could not put his finger on what this odor reminded him of and continued to smell it on himself for days afterwards.

TUBES OF ANTIBIOTIC OINTMENT; (2) 1 oz. tubes of generic pharmacy brand in different stages of flat rolling. K studied and documented data on his body as it begun to mutiny at all levels of organization. *Cellular oxidation, kidney damage, arthritis, asthma, hemorrhoids, eczema.* Folliculitis on his scalp and face made him dream that a giant magnet was pulling all of his hairs, infinite black metal filings, cleanly and discreetly out into the air. The billions of filings would swarm until they found another home elsewhere in the city. The hive would then work day and night to produce an opaque substance that filled a house and started to ooze from the doors and windows. K woke himself up yelling and heard his heart thumping in his ears. Nighttime coughing had progressed to the point where he was forced to sit upright in the armchair to sleep. (There was also the matter of the medical journals stacked over a good portion of the bed surface). Childhood asthma grew worse with age and an increasingly crowded existence. He tried misting the air with water in an occasional effort to weigh down the dust particles, hoping that they would settle on surfaces and stay there, inert.

NYLON FISHING LINE SPOOL; 0.28 mm line, 100 m. Breaking strain: 7.9 kg / 17.4 lb.

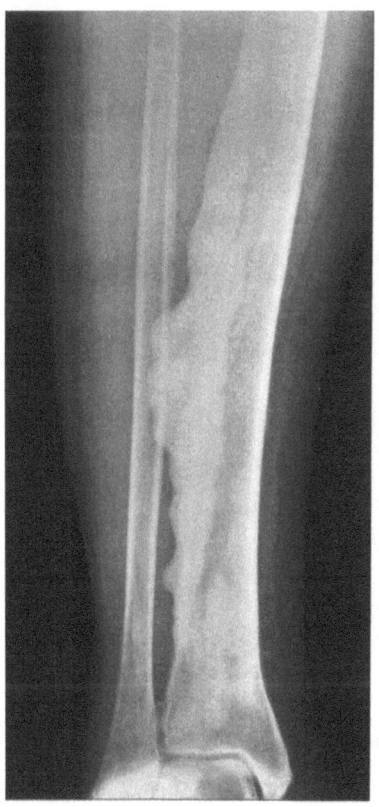

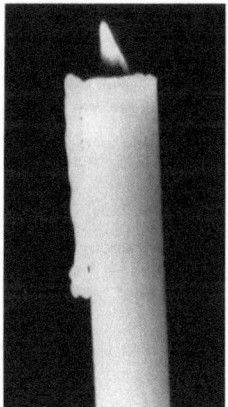

Fig. 9. 'Dripping Candlewax Sign.' Radiograph showing typical 'flowing' bone formation along cortex of tibia.

Quarter-Round Moulding; oak. Unfinished, ready for staining or painting. Used to cover expansion space at wall base and other vertical surfaces.

. . . .

Rotary Phone; goldenrod yellow, the plastic rotary disk also yellowing.

– *Hello?*

– *Hello? Uncle K__?*

– *Who is this?*

– *It's me, Uncle K__, your niece...*

– *Who?*

– *"You mean you don't recognize my voice?*

– *I-er-well, J__?*

– *Yes, it's me! Oh, I'm so glad that you picked up. I'm in a bit of a bind, and you were the only person I could think to call. I was on my way out of town and my car broke down on the Inter-state. I'm in the middle of nowhere. I couldn't call my parents because, well, to be honest, you know how they are and I'm em-barrassed about my situation. I've been meaning to visit them, really, and I will soon, but I was offered a place in line to hug the Guru Maharaji this weekend. A brief trip. And the engine just started smoking out of nowhere, and now it's completely dead. Luckily, the mechanic here says he can fix it in less than a day, and I can be off tomorrow evening. But I just happen to be waiting on a deposit to go through from a job I did a while back and right now am strapped for cash. I was wondering if you could possibly wire some money? I would pay you back as soon as the money I'm expecting comes through, on Friday probably at the latest. And my parents wouldn't have to worry themselves, I know they'd be so worried.*

– What? It died? Are you still driving the...what was it? The old Corolla?

– Yes, ha! you remember it! You're still sharp as a tack. And I can count on you to pick up the phone. You were the only person I can count on to help me out.

– How much did you say you needed?

– I didn't. But it's gonna be $1,200. Guess parts and labor are hard to come by out here.

– Oh, hmmm, well. That's a lot of money.

– I know, but I have money coming in, see, it's just the timing's not very good. There's a Western Union right here, and it'll be a cinch. Here, let me give you the information. I'll have the money back to you by the end of the week.

– Well, I could wire you the money, but there's just one problem...

– Yeah, what is it? I can even pay you back a bit extra for your trouble. It would REALLY help me out.

– The problem is....I don't have a niece.

– Wha-- Uncle K__....you must be confused....

– No, I know perfectly well that I don't have a niece.

Click.

And if I did she wouldn't be driving a Corolla either, since that fool brother and his family only buy domestic cars, K thought. *Nor did he think she would she be hugging a guru, but he couldn't be sure. Nice try, but the cons can prey on the next senile senior citizen.*

Three minutes thirty-two seconds.

Traveler's Choice Hard-Shell Carry-On Wheeled Garment Suitcase; 9 lbs., 24 in. x 15 in. x 10 in. A traditional upright doubling as a garment case. Expandable two-compartment hybrid hard shell luggage made of 1680 denier ballistic fabric, same material used in developing bullet-proof vests for military purposes. Greater rigidity to prevent permanent deformity when under pressure. Recessed quiet wheels glide on sealed ball bearings. Reinforced top and side carry handles.

. . . .

Super Strong Rare Earth Magnets; ⅜ in. diameter, ⅛ in. thick discs of neodymium iron boron (NdFeB). Individual pull force approximately 4 lb. Maximum working temperature 176-degree Fahrenheit (80-degree Celsius).

Body Pillow; 12 lbs, 60 in. x 17 in. For use between the knees to help relieve pressure on the hips. Fluid-proof, nonallergenic, bacteria-, stain- and fire-resistant cover.

Box of Medical Records; patient files for ophthalmology, dermatology, and otolaryngology offices. The clinics were legally allowed to throw these out when they were over seven years old. Photographs, treatment plans, patient information, consent forms. Such intimate knowledge to simply discard. What would all of these individuals make of their bodies and stories becoming shredded paper waste? And if the files weren't properly destroyed? They'd be forever floating in the public ether. K found this cardboard carton abandoned in a janitor's

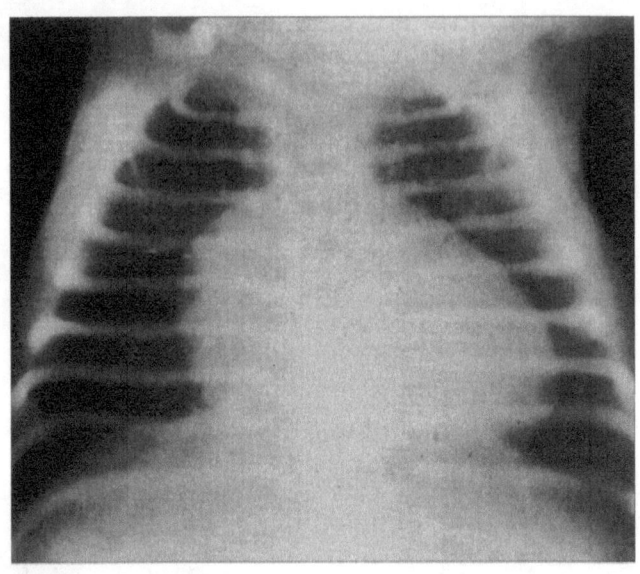

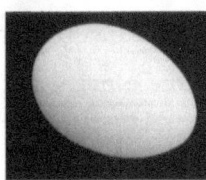

Fig. 9. 'Egg-shaped Heart.' Egg-shaped heart due to 'complete transposition of the great vessels with intact ventricular septum (male, aged 2 days; 1.5 mm patent ductus).'

closet—never even made it to the loading dock for the document destruction company. The box was heavy and required some maneuvering to get onto the wheeled cart from the closet. These files were valuable to K as cases to pore over. Medical images yielded secrets, opened a terrible window into the internal world of the body. Someone with his searching eye and encyclopedic knowledge could examine a radiograph from any part of the body, any type of body, and immediately spot the red flags, suspicious growths, foreign elements. The Unknown quantity "X" in the x-ray was the great equalizer, did not discriminate on the basis of race, sex, age, or creed. Every individual body subject to the penetrating ghostly force of Roentgen's machine yielded its own pattern of electrons escaping absorption. Often as he stared at a person talking to him, he saw them as he read his films, seeing only black, white, and gray. Destruction and diagnosis, same technology. The irony never escaped him. K did not interact with these fragments on film as individuals, never had a face to put to the images, and he preferred it this way. Unreliable accounts of patients could often mislead or obstruct the path to an accurate diagnosis.

Rolls of Receipt Paper; (12) tightly wound around a 1 in. diameter plastic core, held together with a rubber band.

GROMMETS; 103-piece ½ in. grommet installation kit, brass. Useful in repairing old tarps or for customizing a tarp for other purposes, like a secure car cover.

....

FISHER SPACE PEN; still wrote perfectly upside-down, underwater, in extreme heat and cold. A full afternoon spent testing conditions. ZERO-GRAVITY. A prize addition to the pen collection, deserving of prominent display status alongside the Pen-dulum and Pen-and-pencil Libra scales.

4 IN. FLOPPY DISKS; produced in a time when they were no longer floppy. No means to view the data stored on this magnetic tape. *To look into: the history of the technology of memory.*

FM RADIO WITH ATOMIC CLOCK; receiving radio signals from the Official Atomic Clock in Fort Collins, Colorado. Automatic adjustment for daylight savings time. A Public Alert Certified Device.

GOODE'S WORLD ATLAS; Rand McNally, 10th Edition. Cities he could navigate by heart: Seoul, Tokyo, Frankfurt, New York, Los Angeles, Philadelphia, Boston. His granddaughter spent a semester abroad in Tokyo, and his hand-drawn maps of the entire subway system for her consisted of pages of line drawings in blue ink on the backs of letter-size sheets taken from his stash of photocopies, stapled together at the short edge. Knowing her Japanese was at a beginner's level, he wrote in both English and Hiragana. S did not understand why he labored over these. S herself had been to Tokyo with her sister on a two-week guided bus tour, and even though they never once set foot in the subway, S was certain that the hospitality of the culture would provide for a system that was well-mapped, on time, and accessible to foreigners. *They have perfectly good maps there, in color, and for free! What do you think, that they let all the tourists wander around helpless like little babies? Why in the world would she need these?* S never hesitated to insist that K knew nothing about the places he mapped. *Oh, of course, I keep forgetting that you're the expert on overseas travel who has never left the country!* But his granddaughter appreciated them and told him so. He highlighted all of the important lines and transfers. He included all major

57

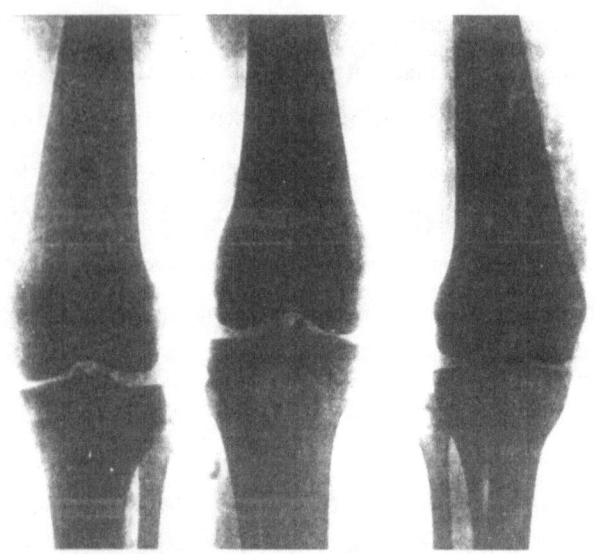

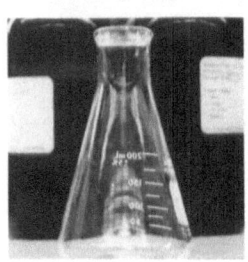

Fig. 10. 'Erlenmeyer Flask Deformity.' Erlenmeyer flask-shaped deformity shown in radiographs of patients with Gaucher's disease and deformity of the distal femur.

hospitals, police stations, the American consulate, banks, tourist information centers, taxi stands. He knew she would be staying in the Ueno area and studying at Waseda University, so the first two pages featured the most efficient route, with warnings about rampant frotteurism at rush hour and about the women-only cars. She wrote to tell him how helpful his maps were, how she carried them around wherever she went and that they were tea-stained but still very legible. He regretted not laminating them. Certainly, carrying around a few stapled pages was much more discreet than walking around with an unwieldy map, looking like a target. K stored her letter safely away with the rest of the correspondence.

Key Rings; (7) in various sizes. Another twentieth century wonder that held the world together. The double loop, a spiral threshold.

Stamp Dispenser; in last Friday's paper, K had read the story of a man who was busily amassing several hundred dollars worth of non-denominated postage. As soon as the postal service had started issuing the Forever stamps, the man had been buying up books, as many as they would allow him. The postal service had raised the rate twice in the last forty-eight months, K noted, for an increase of four cents per first class letter. By his calculation, if they continued the cost increases (and there was every reason to believe they would, with the system going bankrupt) the man's initial investment had yielded at least a 9.5 percent return. At the current rate of increases, in 15 years, the stamps would yield a 400 percent return! And that was not even considering the value of these first issue stamps to future philatelists. *What better government-backed guarantee was there than FOREVER?*

....

MAGNIFYING GLASS; 5 in. diameter, scratched lens that made the sunlight refract light in a complex pattern on the wall. Black plastic handle. Aging eyes and the smallness of print made it harder to read indoors. Wearing glasses gave him a headache, but a magnifying glass equipped with a small light worked well for reading print in the dim lighting. Obstructed windows became a difficulty in the shortened days of winter months. In the summer, the moths, mosquitoes, and flying ants came out of the stacks of paper by the thousands as soon as he turned the light on.

The bugs swarmed so densely that they blocked all of the light from the fixture. He pulled the light switch and sat in the dark for the rest of the night, without even the glow of the television or light table.

Kitchen Step Stool; lightweight, folding to under 2½ in. thin for easy storage. Large top step locked in place, offering a secure and stable standing area. Non-marring feet.

Thin Steel Strip; ⅛ in. x 11 in. x 1/32 in. For years, K had been finding these on the sidewalks and streets, not knowing what they were or where they came from. They were like metal vermicelli or rusted steel tongue scrapers and could be found all across the city, stuck in the concrete expansion joints, in the curb, in the gutters, sitting on the sidewalks. Each one was 1/32 in. thick, made of thin-gauge steel that could be crimped by hand. The one K came across that day was located in front of the county clerk's office where he had been investigating a property appraisal. It was an overcast but blindingly bright morning, and the little metal strip sat there glinting on the sidewalk. As on other occasions, K looked around to see if anyone else noticed him noticing it (they hadn't), and he bent over to pick it up. Eyes squinting and brow furrowed, he puzzled over it. Wondering about the mysterious origin and purpose was one of his mental landmarks as he sat awake in insomnia. His theories, from the feasible to the conspiratorial, all seemed unsatisfactory. At times, he imagined that the unassuming strips were part of a comprehensive, longitudinal study conducted by researchers for environmental or behavioral monitoring and that they were distributed throughout the city as sensors. Perhaps these researchers were trying to collect important data and his own collection was disrupting the study. Then again, no one had come after him. He looked for some trace of chemical coating on them but found nothing. Or perhaps they had to do with some very pragmatic construction method. He knew very little about construction. He already owned a large shoebox-full of the metal strips. They were bundled together with rubber bands by the one-hundreds. A total of forty-eight bundles weighed in at ten pounds eight ounces.

On a Tuesday, in a singular moment that felt like a communiqué from another cosmos, he experienced something as close to religious epiphany as was possible for a man of science.

The answer to his enduring personal mystery came barrelling towards him when he was out walking at an unusual hour. K had heard from a neighbor that a local charity was running a donation drive for un-

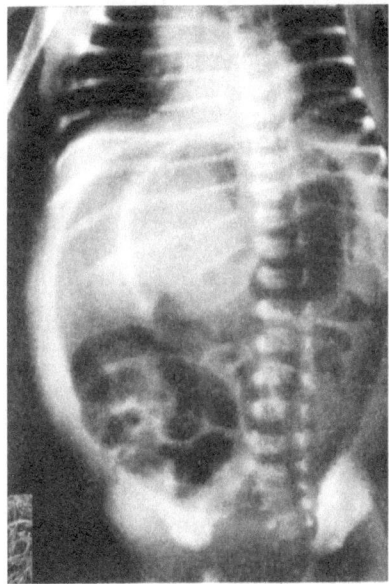

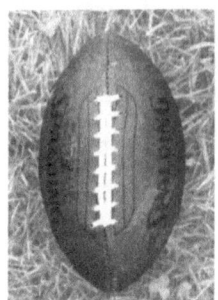

Fig. 11. 'Football Sign.' The football sign seen in a 'three-day-old male with normal forty-week gestation. Although there is slight rotation, the large oval divided superiorly by the streak of the falciform ligament is easily seen.'

wanted electronics and that around the city and that people were putting out their e-waste for curbside pickup. K thought he might see what sorts of things had become obsolete before he himself had ever owned any of them. He walked along a residential street and stopped to peek into a cardboard box full of parts, wires, and boxes entangled in a mass of black plastic. A low rumble from a distance did not register in his awareness as he studied the pile of what he guessed to be orphaned power adapters. The rumble increased to a roaring and noisy whooshing as it came nearer, until it was almost upon him. As he jumped aside, the giant mechanical street sweeper nearly sideswiped him, a jitterbugging monster pawing at the curb and kicking up dirt, rocks, debris. Before he could yell and shake his fist at the driver, LO and BEHOLD, a glint of light came cartwheeling through the air, nicked his left shin, and landed on the sidewalk. He bent over slowly in the fog of dust to pick up the sliver of light. He gasped audibly and slapped his forehead. A BRISTLE! OF COURSE! He felt like Odysseus holding the eyelash of Cyclops and looked around to see if anyone had witnessed the near-accident and revelation (they hadn't). He sat staring at this simple answer to the years of enigma. He should have known that this was a trace of the urban infrastructural sanitation machine. K put the bristle safely and satisfyingly in his inside coat pocket to add to his collection.

VELCRO Heavy-Duty Straps; 2 in. x 6 ft.; blue, great for bundling and securing items of almost any shape or size.

. . . .

Imitation Leather Belts; (2), both black. Made in China. One creased to the point of tearing at the last hole; the other, new or never worn.

Men's Tie; diamonds, hearts, spades, and clubs floating in pattern against a silver paisley background. K thought about Lewis Carroll's Queen of Hearts.

Toy Car; glittering red Corvette with white racing stripe. Chipping paint revealed galvanized metal, a broken rear axle made the rear passenger-side wheel dangle like a loose tooth. K had found this one on the seat of a rush hour train. His thoughts went to the young boy who had been in the train car across the aisle, catty-cornered to him: the boy, who for a split-second, K mistook for his son M at the age of eight. The likeness was so complete that his arm reached out and he started to say something, but he caught himself. He really looked a lot like M—from the underweight frame to the bulge of his forehead and the light eyebrow fuzz that met in the middle. When the boy caught him looking, K gave a crooked smile, which made the boy look down at the muddy floor of the car. K could not stop staring. The boy was sitting against the seat with his backpack on, next to a young mother. His legs were swinging vigorously back and forth so that when the train stopped, they drew overlapping circles instead of parallel lines in the air. He was holding a toy action figure with both of his small hands. Over the course of four stops, he configured it into a car and ran it across his own thighs and then re-configured it into a robot and made slobbery machine gun sounds as he pointed it at the other passengers. He was showing off for the old man who was watching. M would have turned forty-five this year. The boy looked up and smiled slyly.

K stood up abruptly and got off, even though it was not his stop. He began to fight for oxygen; everyone else on the platform was conspiring to consume all of it before him. The air became opaque. His cheeks drained at the same time that the crown of his head felt hot. The sound of the next approaching train should have been getting louder as it approached but was cutting out, a muffled thunder, then silence. K did not feel the impact when his head hit the platform. A week's worth of newspapers he'd been holding under one arm went flying as he fell, and the train whooshed by.

Everyone later kept repeating how very fortunate it was that someone had recognized him. A young resident who had been on his way home after the night shift. K had no identification and he had not been wearing his embroidered white coat. (He had recently convinced himself if that if he was the victim of a kidnapping and attempted extortion, the criminals would not be able to reach his family if he remained unidentifiable and refused to give his name). He woke up in a gown, in a bed behind curtains, with an IV hook-up. The nurse was taking his pulse and temperature (90 BPM; 103.9 degrees Fahrenheit) and when she saw him alert told him that his family had been notified and were on their way. For the first time, he found himself on the receiving end of the medical system he was normally an agent of. He put up mild resistance. The edges of the room were unresolved, and the back of his head was very sore on the right side.

Who knew how long he had been ill. He could remember feeling flush, light-headed, weak. But sleepless nights had the same effect. His daughter-in-law was the first to arrive.

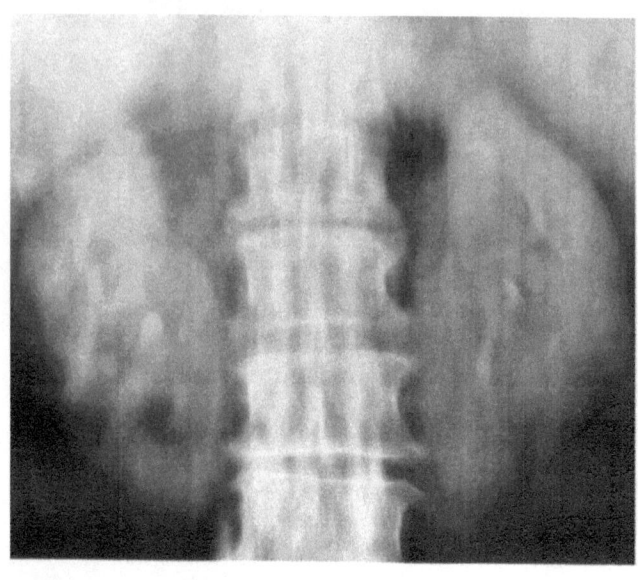

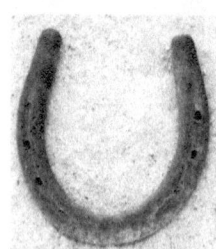

Fig. 12. 'Horseshoe Kidney.' Nephrotomogram of horseshoe kidney.

She rushed into the room and spoke in a low tone that was reserved for scandals involving neighbors or relatives or when things were really serious.

Continuing a conversation with herself, she began muttering in lower tones. He made no response except to close his eyes. The sound of her voice hovered in and out.

After the subway incident, the family was loathe to let him continue living alone, but they had no choice. After three days, his fever subsided, and he was released. He checked himself out and promptly went to the mailroom to catch up on the news he had missed. There was nothing anyone around him could do but watch as he went right back to his routine. No one was so cruel as to try to convince either of them that S should move back in, and he could not be persuaded to move out. And so things returned to normal. If he had acquired any newfound awareness of mortality, he did not show it.

. . . .

¹¹⁄₃₂ IN. DRILL BIT; 4¾ in. long, heavy-duty, for use in wood, metal, plastics, and fiberglass. A no-spin shank eliminates the frustration of bit spinning in the chuck.

MIRROR COMPACT; 4½ in. diameter, imitation opal cover. He first noticed liver spots forming (*solar lentigines*— nothing to do with the liver, of course) on his hands and face at sixty. They were collecting like oil stains in the driveway. A small booklet of face powder had been left by either S or his mother, not sure which. He started using the scented powdery leaflets on the spots one day. More from curiosity than vanity. He had no reference for aging gracefully as a man. Mother had aged all too well. Even after multiple strokes, she had the same flash in her eyes, and her skin stayed taut and luminous. She managed to maintain the same intensity, at the same frequency but with decreasing amplitude, like someone turning the volume knob down for the last movement of the symphony.

His high cheekbones and protruding forehead were becoming sunken around the temples. He noticed how aging was feminizing his looks. He saw his Mother staring back at him. He had never really taken after her— of the three children, his older brother had inherited more of her, phenotypically speaking. The two of them shared the same deep-set eyes, longish nose, demure chin. As K lost weight, her bone structure started to emerge in his own face. His other facial features seemed to be accommodating the change. The latent resemblance startled him.

She had never considered remarrying, to K's knowledge. She continued to live with K and his family throughout the birth of his three sons and their childhood, adolescence, and flight. As long as she was alive, his wife S would not be leaving, of course. The two women busily kept house and took care of the boys together, cooking, cleaning, fussing. Back then, things always seemed to find their place in the house, or they simply disappeared. When a journal or document went missing, he searched and searched until he was forced to ask. He would approach S first. She would declare ignorance and tell him to ask Mother. When he did so, she replied without looking up from whatever she was doing, *It was old, so I threw it out,* or *You don't need that around anymore.* He needn't argue with her.

After Mother's stroke, S tried the same tricks. K argued

that she was liable to throw something very valuable that he had hidden away. She never believed him and simply kept gathering and ordering his things.

Stainless Steel Sheet Metal Screw Assortment Kit; 102 pieces, made from hardened steel. Threads create their own mating thread in pre-drilled holes.

. . . .

Rubber Erasers; the pink, extruded parallelogram of these erasers was a source of endless joy. To imagine the factories where pink liquid poured into open-mouthed molds to produce these perfect shapes! The inked type on smooth rubber was arousing. Just the right mix of absorption and resistance. K could not think of a better form for this function: corners and edges maximized for precision rubbing, with an overall dimension that fit snugly in the palm. It was a great comfort to know that they were being produced in just the same way that had been when he was a grade-schooler, although he could not remember the last time he saw someone else using one. You had to be delicate in order not to break the corners off with these now brittle pieces. Just about every eraser shape had

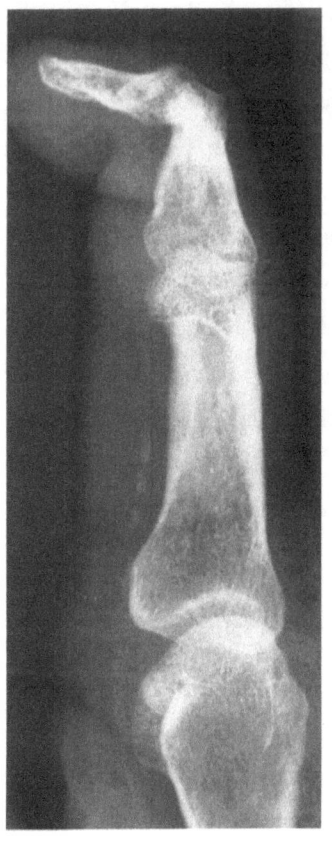

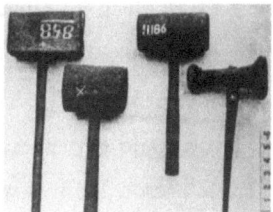

Fig. 13. 'Mallet (Baseball) Finger.' Typical radiographic appearance of mallet finger.'

its own particularly satisfying qualities: *White Triangular Prisms, Gray Blocks with Rounded Edges, Tiny Cylindrical Pellets from Mechanical Pencils.* He remembered collecting and trading these with classmates, so excited when was given an allowance for school supplies that he would lie awake imagining each shape turning in his hand. The ones printed with cartoon animals were highly prized, and you could get at least three or four smaller ones for a lion or parrot. He was willing to sacrifice the animals for quantity. He kept one in hand at school all day, fondling it under the desk. It offered its rubbery reassurance. He would rotate among his collection so as not to favor one over another, careful not to rub away the inked image if there was one. With a sigh, the adult K imagined that these would probably be the next thing to disappear, doomed to the history of Obsolete Stationery Products.

Umbrella; alternating blue, red, and white segments. Automatic push button still sent the canopy flying open with a surprising force and feel of lift. Open to 55 in. diameter.

Umbrella Stand; designed and built by company that offered European-styled housewares to the U.S. market, with early success in ironing and storage; also launched the industry's first line of digital in-oven thermometers, equipped with a long cord so consumers can digitally monitor food without removing it from the oven.

OFFICE CHAIR; what one might call an Executive Chair. Black leather, ergonomic mid-back chair with lumbar support and pneumatic seat height adjustment. Large 27 in. nylon base for greater stability. Hooded double wheel casters; upright locking position and adjustable tilt tension.

PRINT OF CT SCAN; patient with suspected tumor in left kidney. This state-of-the-art imaging was proof of human mastery over the body. The thin slices of clearly demarcated tissue, bone, and cavity were so crisp and resolved, unlike the soft focus of a traditional x-ray. They made an exquisite composite that was tangible, like having the object in hand that could be spun around, palpated, understood. He had read films for so many years that he was a known expert and had retired before the newer technologies came along. After his retirement, he continued to read films, the old-fashioned kind, that private clinics sent by messenger bike. He read in the evenings after his collecting trips in the city. He read ten to twenty films a night, sitting at his study with the light table as the only light source. He was paid by the sheet, at a rate that had not changed for over twenty years, so that what he earned for one sheet of film did not keep pace with the cost of a soda.

CORKSCREW; joints particularly loose, so that its skeletal body rattled. K did not drink wine and very rarely drank other forms of alcohol. After one drink he would start to retch. Despite or because of this, he owned a collection of alcohol surpassing that of any liquor store in the neighborhood in volume and selection. Each had been given to him at holidays and other professional events. An enviable selection of top shelfs sat untouched, gathering dust. Whiskeys were the most numerous (surgeons love to give whiskey), then came scotch, gin, and port. S inevitably cited this collection in her Cassandra-inspired moments of catastrophic vision: *one house-sized Molotov cocktail that will destroy the whole block!* The liquors, along with the papers, books, journals, and objects were major fuel for her fire.

DISPOSABLE SHOWER CAPS; (100) single-use disposable clear plastic caps to protect hair from moisture and wetness or to keep hair dry. One size fits most.

CHRISTMAS TREE STAND; for artificial trees up to 7½ ft. tall.

CAN OPENER; K studied a broad range of can opener designs. He continued to search for a suitable model for arthritic hands.

BIC Razor; how much less frequently he had to shave in recent years. The daily millimeter of facial hair growth had always been more reassuring than a nuisance. Here was a tangible sign of his cells regenerating, his biology industriously humming away. Thinking about the five million follicles of the human body, all of which are in place by the end of the second trimester in a developing fetus, he rubbed shaving cream on his chin. *The body does not add new follicles.* This daily ritual was a reminder that he was still a living, breathing product of cell division and reproduction. And so the slowing of this growth added to the list of disturbing changes. He had never had much to begin with. He was not genetically suited to survive in a cold climate, he thought.

....

NAIL CLIPPERS; for toenails, the kind you worked from an angle perpendicular to the growth. K had a recurring image of someone coming after him with nail clippers. He was unsure if this was a memory or a hallucination from childhood. He tried vigorously to escape the grasp of this person but failed, feeling paralyzed in the end. He sat imprisoned while he or she (indeterminable) pinched each of his toenails and fingernails, clipping away. Every clip caused agony as he was terrified of being cut too close to the skin. Each time, he thought he saw a crescent shaped chunk of his toe or finger go flying. The nightmare manicurist always started always with the left big toe, sometimes making it through all five and then on to the right one. K would shake his head and shudder.

As with shaving, he found he needed to clip his nails less and less frequently, until he just stopped. He could not remember the last time his nails were clipped, because of the fearful scene and because they seemed to have stopped growing at an acceptable length. Longish nails were admittedly a bit of a hassle in handling x-ray film, but they came in handy for other situations such as peeling off the stickers from fruit.

ROLL OF PAINTER'S TAPE; 2 in. x 180 ft., flexible crepe backing design for conformity. Designed to remove clean after fourteen days.

PROFESSIONAL TECHNICAL PEN SET; (4) pens with ink-feed system designed for consistent line width at any angle. Metal pen barrel and four interchangeable points: 0.25 mm, 0.35 mm, 0.50 mm, 0.70 mm. Assortment of colors.

STAINLESS STEEL TEA BALL INFUSER; 2 in. diameter giving tea plenty of room to expand in the ball, for maximum flavor extraction.

SWING ARM LAMP; can be clamped onto surfaces that are vertical or horizontal. Ventilated double shade baffle for glare reduction. Spring-balanced adjustable arm extending to 32 in.

POWER STRIP; six-outlet strip extending the functionality of electrical outlets. Circuit breaker switch for maximum energy conservation when accessories are not in use. Maximum load on six outlets not to exceed 15 amps.

ENCYCLOPAEDIA BRITTANICA COMPLETE 32 VOLUME PRINT SET; hardcover. Volumes 6 through 10 sealed shut by spilled white paint. *"The 84 new articles in this printing include Kerry, John; Nanotechnology; Wal-Mart; Weapons of Mass Destruction (WMD); and Yo-Yo Ma. New articles on Animal rights, Monkey-pox, and SARS update biomedical coverage. Among the 3,900 rewritten or revised articles are African American literature, Great Depression, Mt. Everest, and Vietnam War. More than 120 maps have been added or changed, including those for Chicago, Europe, Iran, Iraq, United Nations Peacekeeping, and Vietnam War. Among the 119 new illustrations are new flag and primate plates."*

Master Padlock/Combination Lock: 9/32 in. shackle diameter, ¾ in. shackle length. 3-step dial code.

Wood Shims; 15 in. long, made from eastern white cedar. Indispensable for projects requiring level, plumb, or square.

Left-Handed Scissors; left blade on top. Specially molded finger grips.

Medical Tuning Fork; extra-long 2 in. handle of turned smooth aluminum; 256 Hz pitch for Rinne bone conduction test.

The Internal Objects
Copyright © 2013 *Future Plan and Program*

Images, pp. 5, 83 by Szu-Han Ho

Images and text on pp. 12, 17, 21, 26, 31, 36, 41, 44, 49, 54, 58, 63, 68, 73 reprinted from Michael E. Mulligan, *Classic Radiologic Signs: an atlas and history* © 1997 by Parthenon Publishing Group: New York.

ISBN: 978-0-9833815-8-7

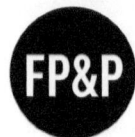

future plan and program

Future Plan and Program
http://futureplanandprogram.com

Please direct inquiries to:
thefuture@futureplanandprogram.com

Series editor: Steffani Jemison
Series designer: Sebastian Civarolo

Future Plan and Program was incubated in 2010-2011 by Project Row Houses.

Special thanks to Kristi McGuire, Katherine Lennard, and Nikki Pressley.

Future Plan and Program was generously funded in part by the following individuals: Kerry Inman & Denby Auble, John Roberson & John Blackmon, Danielle Antoinette Burns, Justin Cavin, Jereann Chaney, Melody Clark, Ashley Clemmer Hoffman & Brendan Hoffman, Phyllis L. McCallum and Steven Jemison, Joey Romano & Nicole Laurent, Victoria Thomas McGhee, Scott Sawyer & Michael Peranteau, Gregory & Diane Schultz, Leigh & Reggie Smith, and Rebecca Trahan. Special thanks to Jill Whitten & Robert Proctor.

Funding for Steffani Jemison's residency at Project Row Houses was provided by: The National Endowment for the Arts, the City of Houston through the Houston Arts Alliance, Houston Endowment Inc., The Brown Foundation, The Kresge Foundation, The Andy Warhol Foundation for the Visual Arts, and the Texas Commission on the Arts. Steffani Jemison's residency was part of a collaboration with the Core Program at the Glassell School of Art of the Museum of Fine Arts Houston.

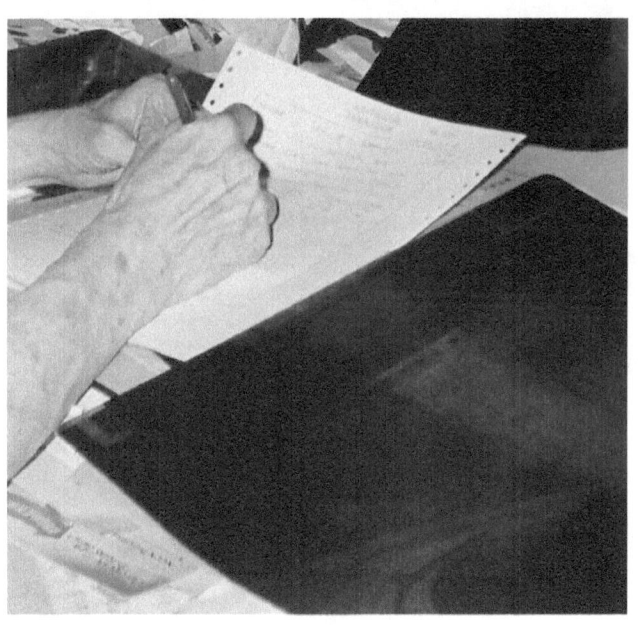